Hieroglyphica Horapollinis,

a Davide Hoeschelio fide Codicis Augustani
ms. correcta, suppleta, illustrata Augustae
Vindelicorum:
ab insigne pinus

of

Michaele Mairo Comite

ARCANA
ARCANISSIMA
HOC EST
HIEROGLYPHICA
ÆGYPTIO-GRÆCA.
Vulgo necdum cognita,
ad demonstrandam falsorum apud anti=
quos deorum, dearum, heroum, animantium
et institutorum pro sacris receptorum, origi=
nem, ex vno Ægyptiorum artificio, quod aureū
animi et Corporis medicamentum peregit, deduc=
tam: Vnde ki pöetarum allegoriæ, scriptorum
narrationes fabulosæ et pertotam Encyclo=
pædiam errores sparsi clarissima veritatis
luce manifestantur, suæq3 tribui
singula restituuntur, sex
libris exposita
Authore
MICHAELE MAIERO COMITE
PALATII CÆSAREI, EQVITE EXEMTO,
Phil: et Med: Doct: et: Cæsar:
Mai: quondam Aulico.

OSIRIS.

TYPHON.

ISIS.

HERCVLES.

DIONYSVS.

IBIS.   APIS.   CYNOCEPHALVS.

3

CONTENTS

The Hieroglyphica

BOOK ONE

1	On Eternity	36	On the Heart
2	On the Universe	37	On Education
3	On the Year	38	On Egyptian Letters
4	On the Month	39	On the Sacred Scribe
5	On the Season	40	On a Magistrate or Judge
6	On what is meant by a Hawk	41	On the Shrine-Bearer
7	On the Soul	42	On the Horoscopist
8	On Ares and Aphrodite	43	On Purity
9	On Marriage	44	On the Lawless or Abominable
10	On the Only Begotten	45	On the Mouth
11	On what is meant by a Vulture	46	On Courage with Temperance
12	On Hephaistus	47	On Hearing
13	On what the Stars Signify	48	On the Penis of a Fecund Man
14	On what a Baboon Signifies	49	On Impurity
15	On Moonrise	50	On Disappearance
16	On the Two Equinoxes	51	On Impudence
17	On Spiritedness	52	On Knowledge
18	On Strength	53	On a Son
19	On Guard	54	On a Fool
20	On Fear	55	On Gratitude
21	On the Rising of the Nile	56	On the Unjust and the Ungrateful
22	On Egypt	57	On Ingratitude for Kindness to Oneself
23	On a Man who has never	58	On the Impossible

Travelled

24 *On Phylacteries*

25 *On an Unformed Man*

26 *On an Opening*
27 *On Speech*

28 *On Silence*

29 *On a Distant Voice*

30 *On Ancient Descent*
31 *On Taste*
32 *On Pleasure*

33 *On Copulation*
34 *On the Soul delaying here a*
    long Time
35 *On the Return of a long-*
    absent Traveller

59 *On a very powerful*
    King
60 *On the King as*
    Guardian
61 *On a Cosmic Ruler*
62 *On the People obedient*
    to the King
63 *On the King Ruling*
    part of the Cosmos
64 *On the Almighty*
    (Pantocrator)
65 *On a Fuller*
66 *On a Month*
67 *On a Plunderer, a*
    Fecund Man, and a
    Madman
68 *On the Rising Sun*
69 *On a Sunset*

70 *On Shadows*

BOOK TWO

1 *On what is meant by a*
   Star
2 *On what is meant by an*
   Eagle's Chick
3 *On what is meant by*
   Two Feet
4 *On what is meant by a*
   Heart & Gullet

5 *On what is meant by*
   Hands, a Shield & Bow

61 *On what is meant by*
    a Basilisk
62 *On what is meant by*
    a Salamander
63 *On what is meant by*
    a Mole
64 *On what is meant by*
    an Ant & Bat's
    Wings
65 *On what is meant by*
    a Beaver

8

6   *On what is meant by a Finger*   66   *On what is meant by Two Monkeys*

7   *On what is meant by a Penis held in a Hand*   67   *On what is meant by a Monkey Urinating*

8   *On what is meant by an Anemone Flower*   68   *On what is meant by a Goat*

9   *On what is meant by the Spine*   69   *On what is meant by a Hyena*

10   *On what is meant by a Quail's Bone*   70   *On what is meant by Two Animal Skins*

11   *On what is meant by Two Men Greeting*   71   *On what is meant by a Hyena facing Two Ways*

12   *On what is meant by a Man in Armour*   72   *On what is meant by a Hyena Skin*

13   *On what is meant by a Man's Finger*   73   *On what is meant by a Wolf's Tail without a Tip*

14   *On what is meant by a Solar Disk cut in Half*   74   *On what is meant by a Wolf & Stone*

15   *On what is meant by a Hawk Flying*   75   *On what is meant by Lions & Torches*

16   *On what is meant by Smoke*   76   *On what is meant by a Lion & Monkey*

17   *On what is meant by a Bull's Horn*   77   *On what is meant by a Bull & Wild Figs*

18   *On what is meant by a Cow's Horn*   78   *On what is meant by a Bull's Bound Knee*

19   *On what is meant by a Bust with a Sword*   79   *On what is meant by Sheep & Goats*

20   *On what is meant by a Hippopotamus*   80   *On what is meant by a Crocodile's Mouth*

21   *On what is meant by a Pair of Stag's Horns*   81   *On what is meant by a Crocodile & Ibis Feather*

22   *On what is meant by a*   82   *On what is meant by*

Dog or Wolf

23 On what is meant by an 83 a Lioness
   Ear

24 On what is meant by a 84 On what is meant by
   Wasp or a Crocodile   a She-Bear

25 On what is meant by a 85 On what is meant by
   Night-Owl   an Elephant's Trunk

26 On what is meant by a 86 On what is meant by
   Snare   an Elephant & Ram

27 On what is meant by 87 On what is meant by
   Words or a Signed   an Elephant & Pig
   Book   On what is meant by
                          a Deer & Viper
28 On what is meant by a 88
   Ladder   On what is meant by
                          an Elephant burying
                          Tusks
29 On what is meant by 89
   Seven Letters, etc   On what is meant by
                          a Dead Crow
30 On what is meant by a 90
   Line on another Line   On what is meant by
                          a Leopard
31 On what is meant by a 91
   Swallow   On what is meant by
                          a Deer & Flute-
                          Player
32 On what is meant by a 92
   Black Dove   On what is meant by
                          an Owl
33 On what is meant by a 93
   Weasel   On what is meant by
                          an Owl & Maiden-
                          hair
34 On what is meant by 94
   Origanum   On what is meant by
                          a Crane on Watch
35 On what is meant by a 95
   Scorpion & Crocodile   On what is meant by
                          Two Partridges
36 On what is meant by a 96
   Marten   On what is meant by
                          an Eagle's Beak
37 On what is meant by a 97
   Pig   On what is meant by
                          Young Crows
38 On what is meant by a 98 On what is meant by

10

	Lion & its Cubs		*a Flying Crane*
39	*On what is meant by a*	99	*On what is meant by*
	Swan		*a Pregnant Hawk*
40	*On what is meant by*	100	*On what is meant by*
	Two Crows		*a Camel*
41	*On what is meant by a*	101	*On what is meant by*
	Blind Beetle		*a Frog*
42	*On what is meant by a*	102	*On what is meant by*
	Mule		*a Frog's Hind Legs*
43	*On what is meant by a*	103	*On what is meant by*
	Bull facing Left, etc		*an Eel*
44	*On what is meant by a*	104	*On what is meant by*
	Dead Horse		*an Electric Ray*
45	*On what is meant by a*	105	*On what is meant by*
	Mare kicking a Wolf		*an Octopus*
46	*On what is meant by a*	106	*On what is meant by*
	Pigeon & Laurel-leaf		*a Lobster & Octopus*
47	*On what is meant by*	107	*On what is meant by*
	Worms		*a Pregnant Lobster*
48	*On what is meant by a*	108	*On what is meant by*
	Pigeon's Hind Parts		*an Oyster & Crab*
49	*On what is meant by an*	109	*On what is meant by*
	Eagle & Stone		*a Scarus Fish*
50	*On what is meant by a*	110	*On what is meant by*
	Horse & Bustard		*a Shark*
51	*On what is meant by a*	111	*On what is meant by*
	Sparrow & Dog-fish		*a Lamprey*
52	*On what is meant by a*	112	*On what is meant by*
	Bat		*a Roach on a Hook*
53	*On what is meant by*	113	*On what is meant by*
	Bat's Teeth & Breasts		*an Octopus Eating*
54	*On what is meant by a*	114	*On what is meant by*
	Turtle-dove		*a Squid*
55	*On what is meant by a*	115	*On what is meant by*
	Cicada		*a Sparrow on Fire*
56	*On what is meant by an*	116	*On what is meant by*

Eagle

57 *On what is meant by a*
    Phoenix

58 *On what is meant by a*
    Stork

59 *On what is meant by a*
    Viper

60 *On what is meant by a*
    Viper also

a Lyre

117 *On what is meant by*
     the Pipes of Pan

118 *On what is meant by*
     an Ostrich Wing

119 *On what is meant by*
     a Man's Hand

APPENDIX I

Cory's Original
PREFACE

For some years past an ardent spirit of enquiry has been awakened with regard to the interpretation of the hieroglyphics inscribed upon the monuments of Egypt. For ages, these had been looked upon as the depositories to which had been committed the religion arts and sciences of a nation once pre-eminent in civilization. Attempts had been continually made to penetrate the darkness, but without the slightest success, till the great discovery of Dr. Young kindled the light, with which the energetic and imaginative genius of Champollion, and the steady industry and zeal of his fellow labourers and successors, have illustrated almost every department of Egyptian antiquity, and rendered the religion and arts, and manners of that country, almost as familiar to us as those of Greece and Rome; and revived the names and histories of the long-forgotten Pharaohs.

The ill success of every previous attempt, may in a great measure, be attributed to the scantyremnants of Egyptian literature that had survived, and the neglect into which the sacred writings of Egypt had fallen, at the time when Eusebius and several of the fathers of the Christian church turned their attention to antiquity.

The ravages of the Persians had scattered and degraded the priesthood of Egypt, the sole depositories of its learning. But the fostering care of the Ptolemies reinstated them in splendour, and again established learning in its ancient seat. The cultivation of the sacred literature and a knowledge of hieroglyphics continued through the whole of the Greek dynasty, although the introduction of alphabetic writing was tending gradually to supersede them. Under the Roman dominion and upon the diffusion of Christianity they further declined; but the names of Roman emperors are found inscribed in hieroglyphic characters, down to the close of the second century, that of Commodus being, we believe, the latest that appears. During the two centuries that succeeded, the influence of Christianity, and the establishment of the Platonic schools at Alexandria, caused them to be altogether neglected.

At the beginning of the fifth century, Horapollo, a scribe of the Egyptian race, and a native of Phænebythis, attempted to collect and perpetuatein the volume before us, the then remaining, but fast fading knowledge of the symbols inscribed upon the monuments, which attested the ancient grandeur of his country. This compilation was originally made in the Egyptian language; but a translation of it into Greek by Philip has alone come down to us, and in a condition very far from satisfactory. From the internal evidence of the work, we should judge Philip to have lived a century or two later than Horapollo; and at a time when every remnant of actual knowledge of the subject must have vanished. He moreover, expressly professes to have embellished the second book, by the insertion of symbols and hieroglyphics, which Horapollo had omitted to introduce; and appears to have extended his embellishments also to the first book. Nevertheless, there is no room to doubt but that the greater portion of the hieroglyphics and interpretations given in that book, as well as some few in the second book, are translated from the genuine work of Horapollo, so far as Philip understood it: but in all those portions of each chapter, which pretend to assign a reason why the hieroglyphics have been used to denote the thing signified, we think the illustrations of Philip may be detected.

In the first stages of hieroglyphical interpretation, this work afforded no inconsiderable light. But upon the whole, it has scarcely received the attention which it may justly claim, as the only ancient volume entirely devoted to the task of unravelling the mystery in which Egyptian learning has been involved; and as one, which in many instances, unquestionably contains the correct interpretations. In the present edition of the work, where any interpretations have been ascertained to be correct, the chapter has been illustrated by the corresponding hieroglyphic. In those cases where the hieroglyphic is mentioned, but an incorrect interpretation assigned, engravings have been given of it, as well as of the hieroglyphic corresponding to such interpretation, wherever these have been ascertained: and they have been inserted in the hope that they may lead persons better acquainted with the subject to discover more accurate meanings than we have been able to suggest.

Among the engravings is inserted a complete Pantheon of the great gods and goddesses of Egypt —Khem, of whom Osiris is a form, is the great deity corresponding to the Indian Siva, and the Pluto of the Greeks—Phtha, of whom Horus is another form, is the Indian Brahma, and Greek Apollo—and Kneph is the counterpart of Vishnu and Jupiter—Isis, of Vesta—Hathor, of Venus—Neith, of Minerva—and Thoth, of whom Anubis is another form, * is the origin of Mercury.

In this edition, the best text that could be found has been adopted, and in no instance has any emendation been hazarded without express authority; and our own suggestions have throughout been inserted in the notes, or within parentheses. And at the end will be found an index of the authors and manuscripts referred to, as well as the celebrated passages of Porphyry and Clemens relating to Hieroglyphical interpretation.

To Lord Prudhoe, at whose request and expense this work has been completed, and by whom also a very considerable part of the illustrations has been furnished, I beg to return my most sincere thanks. To Sir Gardner Wilkinson's published works I am much indebted, as well as to his assistance in the progress of the work; also to the kindness of Messrs. Burton, Bonomi, Sharpe, and

Birch, who have respectively supplied several additional illustrations. But for more convenient reference, I have generally cited Mr. Sharpe's vocabulary, in which are comprised in a condensed form almost all the established discoveries of his predecessors.

The edition of Horapollo by Dr. Leemans has afforded some illustrations, and several of the various readings subjoined; and it is with great pleasure that the reader is referred to chat work for almost every passage contained in ancient authors which has any bearing upon the subject. The kindness of Mr. Bonomi, in executing designs for all the engravings, and of Mr. J. A. Cory, for the frontispiece and plates at the end, I beg with many thanks to acknowledge: and to Mr. I. P. Cory I am indebted for much assistance throughout the whole progress of the work, both in the translation and the notes, and in furnishing many of the illustrations and elucidations of some of the very obscure passages that occur throughout the work; and also for the labour of correcting much of the press, which he undertook for me while unavoidably engaged in other pursuits.

In conclusion, I beg to state, that upon myself must rest the responsibility of all the errors and deficiencies in the work, which I feel convinced cannot but be many; I trust, however, that they will in general be found comparatively unimportant.

Pembroke College, 1840.

First Book

I.01—To denote Eternity they depict the Sun and Moon, because their elements are eternal. But when they would represent Eternity differently, they delineate a Serpent with its tail covered by the rest of its body: the Egyptians call this Ouraius, which in the Greek language signifies Basilisk: And they place golden figures of it round the Gods. The Egyptians say that Eternity is represented by this animal; because of the three existing species of serpents, the others are mortal, but this alone is immortal; and because it destroys any other animal by merely breathing upon it even without biting. And hence, inasmuch as it thus appears to have power over life and death, they place it upon the head of the Gods.

I.02—When they would represent the universe, they delineate a Serpent bespeckled with variegated scales, devouring its own tail; by the scales intimating the stars in the universe. The animal is also extremely heavy, as is the earth, and extremely slippery, like the water: moreover, it every year puts off its old age with its skin, as in the universe the annual period effects a corresponding change, and becomes renovated. And the making use of its own body for food implies, that all things whatsoever, that are generated by divine providence in the world, undergo a corruption into it again.

I.03—When they would represent a *year*, they delineate Isis, *i.e,*. a woman. By the same symbol they also represent the *goddess*. Now Isis is with them a star, called in Egyptian, Sothis, but in Greek Astrocyon, [the Dog' star]; which seems also to preside over the other stars, inasmuch as it sometimes rises greater, and at other times less; sometimes brighter, and at other times not so; and moreover, because according to the rising of this star we show all the events of the ensuing year: therefore not without

19

reason do they call the year Isis. When they would represent the year otherwise, they delineate a Palm Tree [branch], because of all others this tree alone at each renovation of the moon produces one additional branch, so that in twelve branches the year is completed.

I.04—To represent a *month* they delineate a Palm Branch, or, the Moon inverted. A palm branch for the reason before mentioned respecting the palm tree; and the moon inverted, because they say, that, in its increase, when it has come to fifteen degrees, it appears in figure with its horns erect; and in its decrease, after having completed the number of thirty days, it sets with its horns inverted.

I.05—'To represent the *current year*, they depict [with the sign of the year?] the fourth part of an Arura: now the Arura is a measure of land of an hundred cubits. And when they would express a year they say *a quarter* [add the quarter?]: for they affirm that in the rising of the star Sothis, the fourth part of a day intervenes between the (completion of the solar year and the) following rising (of the star Sothis), because the year of the God [the solar year] consists of only 365 days; hence in the course of each tetracterid the Egyptians intercalate an entire day, for the four quarters complete the day.

I.06—When they would signify *God*, or *height*, or *lowness*, or *excellence*, or *blood*, or *victory*, (or *Ares*, or *Aphrodite*,) [Hor or Hathor], they delineate a Hawk. They symbolize by it *God*, because the bird is prolific and long-lived, or perhaps rather because it seems to be an image of the sun, being capable of looking more intently towards his rays than all other winged creatures: and hence physicians for the cure of the eyes use the herb hawkweed: hence also it is, that under the form of a Hawk, they sometimes depict the *sun* as lord of vision. And they use it to denote *height*, because other birds, when they would soar on high, move themselves from side to side, being incapable of ascending

20

vertically; but the hawk alone soars directly upwards. And they use it as a symbol of *lowness*, because other animals move not in a vertical line, but descend obliquely; the hawk, however, stoops directly down upon any thing beneath it. And they use it to denote *excellence*, because it appears to excel all birds—and for *blood*, because they say that this animal does not drink water, but blood—and for *victory*, because it shows itself capable of overcoming every winged creature; for when pressed by some more powerful bird, it directly turns itself in the air upon its back, and fights with its claws extended upwards, and its wings and back below; and its opponent being unable to do the. like, is overcome.

I.07—Moreover, the Hawk is put for the soul, from the signification of its name; for among the Egyptians the hawk is called *Baieth*. and this name in decomposition signifies soul and heart; for the word Bai is the soul, and Eth the heart; and the heart, according to the Egyptians, is the shrine of the soul; so that in its composition the name signifies 'soul enshrined in heart. Whence also the hawk, from its correspondence with the soul, never drinks water, but blood, by which, also, the soul is sustained.

I.08—To denote *Ares* and *Aphrodite* (*Hor* and *Athor*), they delineate Two Hawks; of which they assimilate the male to Ares (Hor), and the female to Aphrodite (Hathor), for this reason, quod ex cæteris animantibus fœmina mari non ad omnem congressum obtemperat, ut in accipitrum genere, in quo etsi tricies in die fœmina a mare comprimatur, ab eo digressa, si inclamata fuerit paret iterum*. Wherefore the Egyptians call every female that is obedient to her husband Aphrodite (Hathor), but one that is not obedient they do not so denominate. For this reason they have consecrated the hawk to the sun: for, like the sun, it completes the number thirty in its conjunctions with the female.

* 'For the other females do not submit to sexual union with the male as the

21

hawk does. For though she is served by the male thirty times in a day, if called by the male, after being withdrawn, she submits again to his desire.'

When they would denote *Ares* and *Aphrodite* (*Hor* and *Athor*) otherwise, they depict Two Crows [ravens?] as a man and woman; because this bird lays two eggs, from which a male and female ought to be produced, and, ([except?] when it produces two males or two females, which, however, rarely happens,) the males mate with the females, and hold no intercourse with any other crow, neither does the female with any other crow, till death; but those that are widowed pass their lives in solitude. And hence, when men meet with a single crow, they look upon it as an omen, as having met with a widowed creature; and on account of the remarkable concord of these birds, the Greeks to this day in their marriages exclaim, *Ekkoki Kori Korone*[1] though unacquainted with its import.

I.09—To denote *marriage*, they again depict Two Crows, on account of what has been mentioned.

I.10—To denote an only begotten, or generation, or a father, or the world, or a man, they delineate a Scarabaeus. And they symbolise by this an *only begotten*, because the scarabaeus is a creature self-produced, being unconceived by a female; for the propagation of it is unique after this manner:—when the male is desirous of procreating, he takes dung of an ox, and shapes it into a spherical form like the world; he then rolls it from the hinder parts from east to west, looking himself towards the east, that he may impart to it the figure of the world, (for that is borne from east to west, while the course of the stars is from west to east): then, having dug a hole, the scarabaeus deposits this ball in the earth for the space of twenty-eight days, (for in so many days the moon passes through the twelve signs of the zodiac). By thus remaining under the moon, the race of scarabaei is endued with life; and upon the nine and twentieth day after having opened the

---

[1] 'Boy, drive away the crow.'

ball, it casts it into water, for it is aware that upon that day the conjunction of the moon and sun takes place, as well as the generation of the world. From the ball thus opened in the water, the animals, that is the scarabaei, issue forth. The scarabaeus also symbolizes *generation*, for the reason before mentioned—and a father, because the scarabaeus is engendered by a *father* only— and the *world*, because in its generation it is fashioned in the form of the world—and a *man*, because there is no female race among them. Moreover there are three species of scarabaei, the first like a cat, and irradiated, which species they have consecrated to the sun from this similarity: for they say that the male cat changes the shape of the pupils of his eyes according to the course of the sun: for in the morning at the rising of the god, they are dilated, and in the middle of the day become round, and about sunset appear less brilliant: whence, also, the statue of the god in the city of the sun is of the form of a cat. Every scarabaeus also has thirty toes, corresponding with the thirty days duration of the month, during which the rising sun [moon?] performs his course. The second species is the two horned and bull formed, which is consecrated to the moon; whence the children of the Egyptians say, that the bull in the heavens is the exaltation of this goddess. The third species is the one horned and Ibis formed, which they regard as consecrated to Hermes [Thoth], in like manner as the bird Ibis.

I.II—To denote a mother, or vision, or boundary, or foreknowledge, or a year, or heaven, or one that is compassionate, or Athena [*Neith*], or *Hera* [*Saté*], or *two drachmas*, they delineate it *a mother*, because in this race of creatures there is no male. Gignuntur autem hunc in modum. Cum amore concipiendi vultur exarserit, vulvam ad Boream aperiens, ab eo velut comprimitur per dies quinque*, during which time she partakes neither of food nor drink, being intent upon procreation. There are also other kinds of birds which conceive by the wind, but their eggs are of use only for food, and not for procreation; but the eggs of the vultures that are impregnated by the wind possess a vital principle. The vulture is used also as a symbol of vision, because it sees more keenly than all other creatures; and by looking towards the west when the sun is in the east, and towards the east when the god is in the west, it procures its necessary food from afar. And it signifies a *boundary* [landmark?] because, when a battle is to be fought, it points out the spot on which it will take place, by betaking itself thither seven days beforehand:—and *foreknowledge*, both from the circumstance last mentioned, and because it looks towards that army which is about to have the greater number killed, and be defeated, reckoning on its food from their slain: and on this account the ancient kings were accustomed to send forth observers to ascertain towards which part of the battle the vultures were looking, to be thereby apprized which army was to be overcome. And it symbolizes a *year*, because the 365 days of the year, in which the annual period is completed, are exactly apportioned by the habits of this creature; for it remains pregnant 120 days, and during an equal number it brings up its young, and during the remaining 120 it gives its attention to itself, neither conceiving nor bringing up its young, but preparing itself for another conception; and the remaining five days of the year, as I have said before, it devotes to another impregnation by the wind. It symbolises also a *compassionate person*, which appears to some to be the furthest from its nature, inasmuch as it is a creature that preys upon all things; but they were induced to use it as a symbol for this, because in the 120 days, during which it brings up its offspring, it flies to no great distance, but is solely engaged about its young and their sustenance; and if during this period it should be without food to give its young, it opens its own thigh, and suffers its offspring to partake of the blood, that they may not perish from want of nourishment:—and *Athena* [*Neith*], and *Hera* [*Saté*], because among the Egyptians Athena [Neith] is regarded as presiding over the upper hemisphere, and Hera [*Saté*] over the lower; whence also they think it absurd to designate the heaven in the masculine, τόν ούρανόν, but represent it in the feminine, τήν ούρανόν, inasmuch as the generation of the sun and moon and the rest of the stars, is perfected in it, which is the peculiar

property of a female. And the race of vultures, as I said before, is a race of females alone, and on this account the Egyptians over any female hieroglyph place the vulture as a mark of royalty [maternity?]. And hence, not to prolong my discourse by mentioning each individually, when the Egyptians would designate any goddess who is a mother, they delineate a vulture, for it is the mother of a female progeny. And they denote by it (οὐρανίαν) *heaven*, (for it does not suit them to say τόν οὐρανόν, as I said before,) because its generation is from thence [by the wind]:—and *two drachmas*, because among the Egyptians the unit [of money] is the two drachmas, and the unit is the origin of every number, therefore when they would denote two drachmas, they with good reason depict a vulture, inasmuch as like unity it seems to be mother and generation.
* 'But they are born in this manner: when the vulture longs for conception, she opens her vagina to the North Wind, and is mounted by him for five days.'

I.12—To denote *Hephæstus* [*Phthah*], they delineate a Scarabaeus and a Vulture, and to denote *Athena* [*Neith*], a Vulture and a Scarabaeus; for to them the world appears to consist both of male and female, (for Athena [Neith] however they also depict a vulture) and; according to them, these are the only Gods who are both male and female.

I.13—When they would symbolise the *Mundane God*, or *fate*, or the *number 5*, they depict a Star. And they use it to denote God, because the providence of God maintains the order by which the motion of the stars and the whole universe is subjected to his government, for it appears to them that without a god nothing whatsoever could endure. And they symbolise by it fate, because even this is regulated by the dispositions of the stars:— and also the number 5, because, though there are multitudes of stars in the heavens, five of them only by their motion perfect the natural order of the world.

I.14—To denote the *moon*, or the *habitable world*, or *letters*, or a *priest*, or *anger*, or *swimming*, they portray a Cynocephalus. And they symbolise the *moon* by it, because the animal has a kind of sympathy with it at its conjunction with the god. For at the exact instant of the conjunction of the moon with the sun, when the moon becomes unillumined, then the male Cynocephalus neither sees, nor eats, but is bowed down to the earth with grief, as if lamenting the ravishment of the moon: and the female also, in addition to its being unable to see, and being afflicted in the same manner as the male, ex genitalibus sanguinem emittit*: hence even to this day cynocephali are brought up in the temples, in order that from them may be ascertained the exact instant of the conjunction of the sun and moon. And they symbolise by it the *habitable world*, because they hold that there are seventy-two primitive countries of the world; and because these animals, when brought up in the temples, and attended with care, do not die like other creatures at once in the same day, but a portion of them dying daily is buried by the priests, while the rest of the body remains in its natural state, and so on till seventy-two days are completed, by which time it is all dead. They also symbolise *letters* by it, because there is an Egyptian race of cynocephali that is acquainted with letters; wherefore, when a cynocephalus is first brought into a temple, the priest places before him a tablet, and a reed, and ink, to ascertain whether it be of the tribe that is acquainted with letters, and whether it writes. The animal is moreover consecrated to Hermes [Thoth], the patron of all letters. And they denote by it a *priest*, because by nature the cynocephalus does not eat fish, nor even any food that is fishy, like the priests. And it is born circumcised, which circumcision the priests also adopt. And they denote by it *anger*, because this animal is both exceedingly passionate and choleric beyond others:—and swimming, because other animals by swimming appear dirty, but this alone swims to whatever spot it intends to reach, and is in no respect affected with dirt.
* 'Emitting blood from her genitals.'

I.15—When they would denote the *renovation of the moon*, they again portray a Cynocephalus in this posture, standing upright, and raising its hands to heaven, with a diadem upon its head; and for the renovation they depict this posture, into which the cynocephalus throws itself, as congratulating the goddess, if we may so express it, in that they have both recovered light.

I.16—Again, to signify the *two Equinoxes* they depict a sitting Cynocephalus, for at the two equinoxes of the year it makes water twelve times in the day, once in each hour, and it does the same also during the two nights; wherefore not without reason do the Egyptians sculpture a sitting Cynocephalus on their Hydrologia (or waterclocks); and they cause the water to run from its member, because, as I said before, the animal thus indicates the twelve hours of the equinox. And lest the contrivance, by which the water is discharged into the Horologium, should be too wide, or on the other hand too narrow, (for against both these caution must be taken, for the one that is too wide, by discharging the water quickly, does not accurately fulfil the measurement of the hour, neither the one that is too narrow, since it lets forth the water little by little, and too slowly,) they perforate an aperture to the extremity of the member, and according to its thickness insert in it an iron tube adapted to the circumstances required. And this they are pleased to do, not without sufficient reason, more than in other cases. They also use this symbol, because it is the only animal that at the equinoxes utters its cries twelve times in the day, once in each hour.

I.17—When they would denote *intrepidity*, they depict a Lion, for he has a great head, and fiery eyeballs, and a round face, and about it hairs like rays in resemblance of the sun; and hence it is, that they place lions under the throne of Horus, intimating the connexion of the animal with the god. And the sun is called Horus from presiding over the Hours.

I.18—To denote strength, they portray the Foreparts of a Lion, because these are the most powerful members of his body.

I.19—To denote a *watchful person,* or even a *guard,* they portray the Head of a Lion, because the lion, when awake, closes his eyes, but when asleep keeps them open, which is a sign of watching. Wherefore at the gates of the temples they have symbolically appropriated lions as guardians.

I.20—To signify the *terrible* they make use of the Same Symbol, because this animal, being the most powerful, terrifies all who behold it.

I.21—To signify the *rising of the Nile,* which they call in the Egyptian language Noun, and which, when interpreted, signifies New, they sometimes portray a Lion, and sometimes Three Large Waterpots, and at other times Heaven and Earth Gushing Forth with Water. And they depict a Lion, because when the sun is in Leo it augments the rising of the Nile, so that oftentimes while the sun remains in that sign of the zodiac, half of the new water [Noun, the entire inundation?] is supplied; and hence it is, that those who anciently presided over the sacred works, have made the spouts [?] and passages of the sacred fountains in the form of lions. Wherefore, even to this day in prayer for an abundant inundation ... And they depict Three Waterpots, or Heaven and Earth Gushing Forth with Water, because they make a waterpot like a heart having a tongue,—like a heart, because in their opinion the heart is the ruling member of the body, as the Nile is the ruler of Egypt, and like [a heart with?] a tongue, because it is always in a state of humidity, and they call it the producer of existence. And they depict three waterpots, and neither more nor less, because according to them there is a triple cause of the inundation. And they depict one for the Egyptian soil, as being of itself productive of water; and another for the ocean, for at the period of the inundation, water flows up from it into Egypt; and the third to symbolise the rains which prevail in the southern parts of Ethiopia at the time of the rising of the Nile. Now that Egypt generates the water, we may deduce from this, that in the rest of the earth the inundations of the rivers take place in the winter, and are caused by frequent rains; but the country of the Egyptians alone, inasmuch as it is situated in the middle of the habitable world, like that part of the eye, which is called the pupil, of itself causes the rising of the Nile in summer.

I.22—To designate *Egypt*, they depict a Burning Censer and a Heart. Above it, implying, that as the heart of a jealous person is constantly inflamed, so Egypt from its heat perpetually vivifies the things which are in or near it.

I.23—To symbolize *a man that has not travelled out of his own country*, they delineate an Onocephalus [creature with an ass's head], because he is neither acquainted with history, nor conversant with foreign affairs.

I.24—When they would denote an *amulet*, they portray Two Human Heads, one of a male looking inwards, the other of a female looking outwards, (for they say that no demon will interfere with any person thus guarded); for without inscriptions they protect themselves with the two heads.

I.25—To denote an imperfect man, they delineate a Frog, because it is generated from the slime of the river, whence it occasionally happens that it is seen with one part of a frog, and the remainder formed of slime, so that should the river fall, the animal would be left imperfect.

I.26—When they would denote an *opening*, they delineate a Hare, because this animal always has its eyes open.

I.27—To denote *speech* they depict a Tongue, and a Bloodshot Eye; because they allot the principal parts of speech to the tongue, but the secondary parts thereof to the eyes. For these kinds of discourses are strictly those of the soul varying in conformity with its emotions; more especially as they are denominated by the Egyptians as different languages. And to symbolize *speech* differently, they depict a Tongue and a Hand Beneath; allotting the principal parts of speech to the tongue to perform, and the secondary parts to the hand as effecting the wishes of the tongue.

I.28—To denote *dumbness,* they depict the number 1095, which is the number of days in the space of three years, the year consisting of 365 days, within which time, if a child does not speak, it chews that it has an impediment in its tongue.

I.29—When they would symbolise a voice *from a distance,* which is called by the Egyptians Ouaie, they portray the Voice of the Air, *i.e.,* Thunder, than which nothing utters a greater or more powerful voice.

I.30—To denote *ancient descent* they depict a Bundle of Papyrus, and by this they intimate the *primeval* food; for no one can find the beginning of food or generation.

I.31—To denote *taste* they delineate the Extremity of the Gullet, for all taste is preserved thus far: I am speaking however of *perfect taste.* But to denote *imperfect taste* they delineate the Tongue upon the Teeth, inasmuch as all taste is effected by these.

I.32—When they would represent *delight* they depict the Number 16; for from this age men begin to hold commerce with women, and to procreate children.

I.33—To denote *sexual intercourse* they depict Two Numbers 16. Cum enim sedecim voluptatem esse diximus; congressus autem, duplici constet, maris ac fœminæ, voluptate, propterea alia sedecim adscribunt[2].

I.34—When they would denote a *soul continuing a long time here*, or an *inundation*, they depict the Phoenix the bird: and they denote the *soul* by it, because this is the longest lived of all creatures in the world; and an *inundation*, because the Phoenix is a symbol of the sun, than which nothing is greater in the universe. For the sun passes over all and scrutinises all, hence he is called ... Polys (much).

I.35—To denote a man returning home after a long time from a foreign land they again delineate the Phoenix the bird: for this creature, after an interval of 580 years, when the time of death is about to overtake him, returns to Egypt, and as soon as he pays the debt of nature in Egypt, he is mystically served with funeral rites; and whatever rites the Egyptians pay to the rest of the sacred animals, the same are due to the Phoenix: for it is said by the Egyptians to rejoice in the sun more than other birds, and because among them the Nile overflows through the heat of this god; of which matter we discoursed with you a short time since.

I.36—When they would denote the *heart* they delineate the Isis; for this animal is consecrated to Hermes [Thoth], the lord of every heart and of reasoning. The Ibis also is itself in its own shape like the heart, respecting which great discussions are maintained by the Egyptians.

I.37—To denote *education* they represent the Heaven Distilling Dew, intimating that as falling dew alights on all Vegetables, and softens those which have a nature susceptible of being softened,

---

[2] 'For we say that children are born of pleasure. And since sexual intercourse consists in the pleasure of both partners—that of the man and the woman— they add the numbers 16 together.'

but is unable to operate upon those which essentially remain hard in the same way as upon the others; so also among men education is common to all; and a man of an apt disposition receives it as dew, while a man of a disposition less docile is incapable of doing so.

I.38—To denote the *Egyptian letters*, or a *sacred scribe*, or a *boundary*, they delineate Ink, and a Sieve, and a Reed, and they thus symbolise the Egyptian *letters*, because by means of these things all writings among the Egyptians are executed: for they write with a reed and nothing else: and they depict a Sieve, because the sieve being originally an instrument for making bread is constructed of reed; and they thereby intimate that every one who has a subsistence should learn the letters, but that one who has not should practise some other art. And hence it is that among them education is called *Sbo*, which when interpreted signifies sufficient food. Also they symbolize by these a *sacred scribe*, because he judges of life and death. For there is among the sacred scribes a sacred book called *Ambres*, by which they decide respecting any one who is lying sick, whether he will live or not, ascertaining it from the recumbent posture of the sick person. And a *boundary*, because he who has learnt his letters has arrived at a tranquil harbour of existence, no longer wandering among the evils of this life.

I.39—And again when they would denote a *sacred scribe,* or a *prophet*, or an *embalmer*, or the *spleen*, or *smelling*, or *laughter*, or *sneezing*, [or *government*, or a *judge*,] they depict a Dog. And by this they denote a *sacred scribe*, because it is necessary for one who is desirous of becoming a perfect sacred scribe to be extremely careful, and to bark perpetually, and to be fierce, fawning upon no one, like dogs. And they symbolise by it a *prophet*, because the dog gazes intently ɪ upon the images of the gods more than all other animals, as does a prophet. And an *embalmer* of the sacred animals, because he also surveys the naked and dissected forms which are preserved by him. And the *spleen*, because this animal alone of all other creatures has this organ very light: and whether death or madness seizes him it arises from his spleen. And those who attend this animal in his exequies, when about themselves to die, generally become splenetic; for smelling the exhalations from the dog, when dissecting him, they are affected by them.

And it denotes smelling, and laughter, and sneezing, because the thoroughly splenetic are neither able to smell, nor laugh, nor sneeze.

I.40—When they denote government, or a judge, they place close against the dog a Royal Robe, the undress garment: because like the dog, who, as I said before, gazes intently on the images of the gods, so likewise the minister, being in the more ancient times a judge also, used to see the king naked, and on this account they add the royal garment.

I.41—To signify the *bearer of the shrine*, they depict the Keeper of a House, because by him the temple is guarded.

I.42—To signify an Horoscopus [observer of the hours], they delineate a Man Eating the Hours, not that the man eats the hours, for that is impossible, but because food is prepared for men according to the hours.

I.43—To represent *purity* they delineate Fire and Water, because by these elements all purification is perfected.

I.44—To denote a *thing unlawful*, or an *abomination*, they delineate a Fish, because the feeding upon fish is considered in the sacred rites as abominable, and a pollution: for every fish is an animal that is a desolator [laxative as food?], and a devourer of its own species.

I.45—To represent the *mouth* they depict a Serpent, because the serpent is powerful in no other of its members except the mouth alone.

I.46—To denote *manliness combined with temperance*, they delineate a Bull that has a vigorous constitution[3]. Calidissimum enim est huic animali membrum, ita ut semel eo in fœminæ vulvam immisso, vel absque ullo motu semen effutiat. Quod si quando a vulvâ vaccæ aberrans, in alium corporis partem membrum intenderit, tum ejus immodicâ intentione vaccani vulnerat. Quin et temperans est: quippe cum nunquam post conceptum, vaccam ineat[4].

I.47—To denote *hearing*, they delineate the Ear of the Bull, for when the cow is desirous of conception, (and she continues so for not longer than three hours together,) she vehemently lows, and if during this time the bull should not approach her, she reserves herself till another meeting. This however rarely happens; for the bull hears her from a great distance, and knowing that she is inflamed, he hastens to the meeting, and is the only animal that does so.

I.48—To denote the *member of a prolific man*, they depict a Goat, and not a bull: ille enim antequam annum attigerit, coire non solet: hic septem statim post ortum diebus congreditur,

---

[3] 'A Bull that has an erect member.'

[4] 'For this animal's genital organ is the most hot; by inserting his member once and with hardly any motion into the female, he ejaculates his seed. But if by chance there is a mistake and he thrusts his organ into some other part of the cow's anatomy, then he wounds her with overpowering force. But, on the other hand, he is temperate on account of never entering the female after she has conceived.'

infœcundum et genituræ minime accommodum semen excernens. Prius tamen ac celerius cæteris animantibus coit.[5]

I.49—To denote impurity, they delineate an Oryx (a species of wild goat), because when the moon rises, this animal looks intently towards the goddess and raises an outcry, and that, neither to praise nor welcome her; and of this the proof is most evident, for it scrapes up the earth with its fore legs, and fixes its eyes in the earth, as if indignant and unwilling to behold the rising of the goddess. And it acts in the same manner at the rising of (the divine star) the sun. Wherefore the ancient kings, when the Horoscopus apprised them of the rising of the moon, placed themselves near this animal, and by observing the middle of its operations, ascertained, as by a kind of gnomon, the exact time of the rising. And hence the priests, of all other cattle, eat this alone without being previously marked with the seal, inasmuch as it appears to entertain a kind of aversion to the goddess: and in the desert wherever it finds a watering place, after having drunk, it stirs it up with its lips, and mingles the mud with the water, and throws dust into it with its feet, that it may be fit for no other animal to drink; so malicious and odious has the nature of the Oryx been considered. Nor does it act thus unmeaningly, because it is this same goddess who germinates and causes all things whatsoever to increase that are useful in the world.

I.50—To denote a disappearance, they delineate a Mouse, because it pollutes and spoils all things by nibbling them. They also make use of the same symbol when they would denote discernment, for when many different sorts of bread lie before him, the mouse selects the purest from among them and eats it. And hence the selection by the bakers is guided by mice.

---

[5] 'For the bull cannot serve a cow before he is a year old, but the goat mounts the female seven days after birth, ejaculating a sterile and empty sperm. Yet, nevertheless, it matures before all other animals.'

I.51—To denote *impudence*, they represent a Fly, for this, though perpetually driven away, nevertheless returns.

I.52—To represent *knowledge*, they delineate an Ant, for whatever a man may carefully conceal, this creature obtains a knowledge of: and not for this reason only, but also because beyond all other animals when it is providing for itself its winter's food, it never deviates from its home, but arrives at it unerringly.

I.53—When they would denote a *son*, they delineate a Chenalopex (a species of goose). For this animal is excessively fond of its offspring, and if ever it is pursued so as to be in danger of being taken with its young, both the father and mother voluntarily give themselves up to the pursuers, that their offspring may be saved; and for this reason the Egyptians have thought fit to consecrate this animal.

I.54—When they depict a Pelican, they signify both a *fool*, and an *idiot*, because although like other winged creatures it is able to deposit its eggs on the higher places, it does not, but it merely scrapes up the earth and there lays its eggs. And the people observing this, surround the place with dried cows' dung, to which they apply fire. And when the pelican sees the smoke, by endeavouring to extinguish the fire with its wings, she on the contrary kindles it by their motion: and thus, her wings being burnt by the fire, she easily becomes a prey for the fowlers. And because it enters into the contest simply for the sake of its young, the priests consider it unlawful to eat it. But the rest of the Egyptians eat it, alleging that the pelican does not enter into the contest with discretion, as do the geese, but with folly.

I.55—To represent *gratitude*, they delineate a Cucupha, because this is the only one of dumb animals, which, after it has been brought up by its parents, repays their kindness to them when they are old. For it makes them a nest in the place where it was brought up by them, and trims their wings, and brings them food, till the parents acquire a new plumage, and are able to assist themselves: whence it is that the Cucupha is honoured by being placed as an ornament upon the sceptres of the gods.

I.56—To symbolize an *unjust* and *ungrateful* man, they depict Two Claws of an Hippopotamus turned downwards. For this animal when arrived at its prime of life contends in fight against his father, to try which is the stronger of the two, and should the father give way he assigns him a place of residence, permitting him to live, and consorts himself with his own mother; but if his father should not permit him to hold intercourse with his mother, he kills him, being the stronger and more vigorous of the two. And they make use of the lowest parts of the hippopotamus, the two claws, that men seeing this, and understanding the story of it, may be more inclined to kindness.

I.57—To signify a *man that is ungrateful and quarrelsome with his benefactors*, they delineate a Dove, for when the male becomes the stronger, the drives his father away from his mother, and mates himself with her. This creature however seems to be pure, because when any pestilential epidemic rages, and every thing, animate and inanimate, sickens with disease, those persons alone who feed upon this bird do not share in so great a calamity. Wherefore during such a time nothing is served up to the king as food except the dove alone. And the same food is served up to those who are under a course of purification, that they may minister to the gods. It is likewise reported that this creature has no gall.

I.58—To signify an *impossibility*, they represent a Man's Feet Walking on the Water; or when they would signify the same thing differently, they delineate a Headless Man Walking. And since these are both impossibilities, they have with good reason selected them for this purpose.

I.59—To denote *a very bad* [a very good? a very powerful?] king, they depict a Serpent in the form of a circle, whose tail they place in his mouth, and they write the name of the king in the middle of the coil, intimating that the king governs the world. The serpent's name among the Egyptians is Meisi.

I.60—And otherwise to denote a *vigilant king*, they depict the Serpent (upon the watch), and in the place of the king's name they depict a watcher: for he is the guardian of the whole world; and the king ought to be vigilant everywhere.

I.61—Again when they would signify and designate a *king who rules the world*, they delineate the same Serpent, and in the middle thereof they represent a Large House, and with reason for the royal abode from him ... in the world.

I.62—To denote a *people obedient to their king*, they depict a Bee for this is the only one of all creatures which has a king whom the rest of the tribe of bees obey, as men serve their king. And they intimate from the honey's ... from the force of the creature's sting ... that ... should be both lenient and firm in ... and administration.

I.63—When they would symbolize a *king who governs not all but a part of the world*, they depict Half a Serpent. For by this creature they denote a king, and by half of it, that he is not king over all the world.

I.64—They symbolize *one who governs all things* by the perfect form of the same animal, again depicting the Entire Serpent: for amongst them it is the spirit that pervades the universe.

I.65—To denote a *fuller*, they depict the Two Feet of a Man in Water, and they depict this from the resemblance of the work.

I.66—To represent a *month,* they depict as before explained the figure of the Moon when it has attained the age of eight and twenty days of equal lengths, each day containing twenty-four hours, for during these it is apparent, and in the remaining two it is in a state of evanescence.

I.67—When they would symbolize a *rapacious,* or *prolific,* or *furious man,* they delineate a Crocodile, because it is prolific [?], and fertile in offspring, and furious. For if it fails in its intention of seizing any thing it rages in anger against itself.

I.68—To express *sunrise* they depict the Two Eyes of a Crocodile, because of the whole body of the animal its eyes glare conspicuously from the deep.

I.69—To denote *sunset,* they represent a Crocodile Tending Downwards, for this animal is self productive [?] and inclining downwards.

I.70—To denote *darkness,* they represent the Tail of a Crocodile, for by no other means does the crocodile inflict death and destruction on any animal which it may have caught, than by first striking it with its tail, and rendering it incapable of motion: for in this part lies the strength and power of the crocodile. And now, though there are other appropriate symbols deducible from the nature of the crocodile, those which we have mentioned are sufficient for the first Book.

Here begins the Second Book of Horapollo of Niliacus
on the Interpretation of the
Egyptian Letters.

Now, in this Second Book I will set forth a sound account of what remains. Note also, that I have added things said before by others without explanation.

2.01—When a Star is depicted by the Egyptians, it sometimes symbolizes *God*, sometimes evening, sometimes *night*, sometimes *time*, and sometimes the *soul* of a male man.

2.02—An Eaglet symbolizes something *prolific of males*, or *of a circular form*, or the seed of man.

2.03—Two Feet Conjoined and Advancing, symbolize the *course of the sun in the winter solstice*.

2.04—The Heart of a Man Suspended by the Windpipe signifies the *mouth of a good man*.

2.05—The Hands of a Man, one Holding a Shield and the Other A Bow, when delineated, denote the *front of battle*.

2.06—A Finger denotes *the stomach of a man*.

2.07—Penis manu Compressa[6] denotes *continence in a man*.

---

[6] 'A penis restrained by a hand.'

2.08—The Flowers of the Anemony denote *disease of a man.*

2.09—When we would denote *the loins or the constitution of a man* we depict the Backbone; for some hold that the seed proceeds from thence.

2.10—The Bone of a Quail when delineated symbolizes permanency and safety; because the bone of this animal is difficult to be affected.

2.11—Two Men Joining their Right Hands denote *concord.*

2.12—An Armed Man Shooting with a Bow denotes a *crowd* [troop or army?].

2.13—The Finger of a Man denotes admeasurement.

2.14—When they would denote a *woman pregnant,* they portray the Orb of the Sun with a Star and the Sun's Disk Bisected.

2.15—A Hawk soaring on high towards the east, signifies the *winds;* [the spirit or soul?] and again otherwise, a Hawk with its wings expanded in the air symbolizes the wind, as having wings.

2.16—Smoke ascending towards heaven denotes *fire.*

2.17—A Bull's Horn when depicted signifies *work.*

2.18—A cow's Horn when depicted signifies punishment.

2.19—A Bust portrayed with a Sword denotes impiety.

2.20—A River Horse when delineated, denotes *an hour.*

2.21—A Stag shoots its horns every year, and when depicted, signifies anything of *long duration.*

2.22—A Wolf or a Dog Averted denotes *aversion*.

2.23—An Ear when delineated symbolizes *a future act*.

2.24—A Wasp Flying in the Air signifies either the noxious *blood of a crocodile*, or a *murderer*.

2.25—A Night Raven signifies *death;* for it suddenly pounces upon the young of the crows by night, as death suddenly overtakes men.

2.26—A Noose denotes *love* as ...

2.27—Words and Leaves of a Sealed Book denote *the most ancient*.

2.28—A Ladder signifies a *siege* by reason of its inequality [?].

2.29—Seven Letters included within Two Fingers [Rings?] symbolize a *song*, or *infinite*, or *fate*.

2.30—A straight line with a curved line above it signifies Ten Plane Lines.

2.31—When they would signify that *the whole of a parent's substance has been left to the sons*, they depict a Swallow. For she rolls herself in the mud, and builds a nest for her young, when she is herself about to die.

2.32—When they would symbolise *a woman who remains a widow till death*, they depict a Black Dove; for this bird has no connexion with another mate from the time that it is widowed.

2.33—When they would represent *a man that is feeble, and unable of himself to help himself, but who does so by the aid of others*, they delineate an Ichneumon. For this animal, when it spies a serpent, does not at once attack it, but by its noise calls others to its assistance, and then attacks the serpent.

2.34—When they would symbolise the *departure of ants*, they engrave Origanum. For if this plant be laid down over the spot from whence the ants issue forth, it causes them to desert it.

2.35—When they would symbolise *one enemy engaging with another equal to himself*, they depict a Scorpion and a Crocodile. For these kill one another. But if they would symbolise *one who is hostile to, and has slain another*, they depict a Crocodile or a Scorpion; and if he has slain him *speedily*, they depict a Crocodile, but if *slowly*, a Scorpion, from its tardy motion.

2.36—When they would symbolise *a woman performing the works of a man*, they depict a Weasel; quod maris pudendum habeat velut ossiculum[7].

2.37—When they would symbolise a filthy man, they depict a Hog; from such being the nature of the hog.

2.38—If they would represent *immoderate anger*, so that he who is angry takes a fever thereby, they depict a Lion Breaking the Bones of its own Whelps. And they portray the lion to signify anger, and the whelps having their bones broken, because the bones of the whelps when struck together emit sparks of fire.

2.39—When they would symbolise an *old minstrel*, they depict a Swan, for when old it sings the sweetest melody.

---

[7] 'For the female of this animal has sexual parts like a small bone.'

2.40—When they would symbolise *a man living in intercourse with his own wife*, they depict Two Crows; for these birds cohabit with one another in the same manner as does a man by nature.

2.41—When they would symbolise *a man who has caught a fever from a stroke of the sun, and died in consequence*, they portray a Blind Beetle; for this creature dies after it has been blinded by the sun.

2.42—When they would symbolise *a barren woman*, they delineate a Mule; for this animal is barren, quod matricem rectam non habet.[8]

2.43—When they would symbolise a woman who has brought forth female infants first, they delineate a Bull inclining towards the Left: and again if male infants, then they delineate a Bull inclining to the right. Is enim ex congressu discedens, si ad lævam conversus fuerit, genitam esse fœminam indicat, si ad dexteram marem.[9]

2.44—When they would denote *wasps*, they depict a Dead Horse; for many wasps are generated from him when dead.

2.45—When they would symbolise *a woman who miscarries*, they depict a Mare Kicking a Wolf; for not only by kicking a wolf does a mare miscarry, but it immediately miscarries if it should merely tread on the footstep of a wolf.

2.46—When they would symbolize *a man who cures himself by an oracle*, they delineate a Wood Pigeon carrying a Branch of Laurel; for this bird when sick deposits a branch of laurel in its nest, and recovers.

---

[8] 'Because its uterus is not straight.'

[9] 'For if that animal after mating moves off to the left, its offspring will be female. But if it moves to the right it will produce males.'

2.47—When they would represent *many gnats swarming together*, they depict Maggots; for from them gnats are engendered.

2.48—When they would symbolise *a man who has naturally no bile but receives it from another*, they depict a Dove with her Hinder Parts erect; for in them she has her bile.

2.49—When they would symbolise *a man who dwells securely in a city*, they depict an Eagle Conveying a Stone; for he takes up a stone, either from the sea or land, and deposits it in his nest, to keep it steady.

2.50—When they would symbolise *a man that is weak and persecuted by a stronger*, they delineate a Bustard and a Horse; for this bird flies away whenever it sees a horse.

2.51—When they would denote *a man who flees for refuge to his patron, and receives no assistance*, they depict a Sparrow and an Owl; for the sparrow when pursued betakes itself to the owl, and being near it is seized.

2.52—When they would symbolise *a man who is weak and audacious*, they portray a Bat, for she flies though destitute of feathers.

2.53—When they would represent *a woman suckling and bringing up her children well*, they again portray a Bat with Teeth and Breasts; for this is the only winged creature which has teeth and breasts.

2.54—When they would symbolise *a man fond of dancing and piping*, they delineate a Turtle Dove; for it is taken by means of a pipe and dancing.

2.55—When they would symbolise *a mystic man, and one initiated*, they delineate a Grasshopper; for he does not utter sounds through his mouth, but chirping by means of his spine, sings a sweet melody.

2.56—When they would symbolise *a king who keeps himself apart, and shows no mercy to delinquencies*, they depict an Eagle; for he builds his nest in desert places, and flies higher than all birds.

2.57—When they would denote *the great cyclical renovation*, they portray the bird Phoenix. For when he is produced a renovation of things takes place, and he is produced in this manner. When the Phoenix is about to die, he casts himself vehemently upon the ground, and is wounded by the blow, and from the ichor, which flows from the wound, another Phoenix is produced; which as soon as it is fledged, goes with his father to the city of the sun in Egypt; who when he is come thither, dies in that place at the rising of the sun. And after the death of his father, the young one departs again to his own country; and the priests of Egypt bury the Phoenix that is dead.

2.58—When they would denote *a man fond of his father*, they depict a Stork; for after he has been brought up by his parents he departs not from them, but remains with them to the end of their life, taking upon himself the care of them.

2.59—When they would symbolise *a woman that hates her own husband*, and designs his death, and is complaisant only during intercourse, they delineate a Viper; for when in connexion with the male, she places his mouth in her mouth, and after they have disjoined, she bites the head of the male and kills him.

2.60—When they would denote *children plotting against their mothers*, they delineate a Viper; for the viper is not brought forth in the [usual manner?], but disengages itself by gnawing through the belly of its mother.

2.61—When they would symbolise *a man who is reproached with accusations and thence falls sick*, they delineate a Basilisk; for he kills those that approach him with his breath.

2.62—When they would symbolise *a man that is burnt with fire*, they depict a Salamander; for it destroys with either head.

2.63—When they would symbolise *a blind man*, they depict a Mole; for it neither has eyes, nor does it see.

2.64—When they would symbolise *a man that never stirs out*, they depict an Ant and the Wings of a Bat; because, when these wings are placed over an ant's nest, none of them come forth.

2.65—When they would symbolise *a man injured by self inflictions*, they delineate a Beaver; for when pursued he tears out his own testicles, and casts them as spoil to his pursuers.

2.66—When they would symbolise a *man who has been succeeded in his property by a son whom he hated*, they depict an Ape with a Young Ape Behind It, For the ape begets two young apes, one of which he loves extravagantly, and the other he hates: and the one which he loves he keeps before him and kills with fondling; but the one which he hates he keeps behind him and brings up.

2.67—When they would symbolise *a man that conceals his own defects*, they depict an Ape Making Water; for when he makes water he conceals his urine.

2.68—When they would symbolise *a man who hears with more than usual acuteness*, they portray a She-Goat, for she respires [hears?] through both her nostrils and ears.

2.69—When they would symbolise *one that is unsettled*, and that does not remain in the same state, but is sometimes strong, and at other times weak, they depict an Hyena; for this creature is at times male, and at times female.

2.70—When they would symbolise *a man overcome by his inferiors*, they depict Two Skins, one of an Hyena, and the other of a Panther; for if these two skins be placed together, the panther's shoots its hair, but the other does not.

2.71—To denote *a man who overcomes his private enemy*, they delineate an Hyena turning to the Right; but if *himself overcome*, they on the contrary depict One turning to the Left; for should this animal, when pursued, turn to the right, it slays the pursuer, but if to the left, it is slain by the pursuer.

2.72—When they would indicate a 'man unaffected by evil', especially one who passes through travail fearlessly even until death, they draw the skin of a hyena, for if a man should wrap this skin about his body he will pass through all of his enemies uninjured and fearlessly.

2.73—When they would represent *a man annoyed by his private enemies, and extricating himself with small loss*, they portray a Wolf which has Lost the Extremity of his Tail; for the wolf, when about to be hunted, shoots the hairs and extremity of his tail.

2.74—When they would denote a man who is fearful lest accidents should happen unexpectedly to himself, they depict a

Wolf and a Stone; for it fears neither iron, nor a stick, but a stone only; and indeed, if any one throw a stone at him he will find him terrified: and wherever a wolf is struck by a stone, maggots are engendered from the bruise.

2.75—When they would denote *a man calmed by fire even during anger*, they portray Lions and Torches; for the lion dreads nothing so much as lighted torches, and is tamed by nothing so readily as by them.

2.76—When they would denote *a feverish man who cures himself*, they depict a Lion Devouring an Ape; for if, when in a fever, he devours an ape, he recovers.

2.77—When they would denote *a man who after his former excesses at length becomes steady*, they portray a Bull Bound about by a wild Fig Branch; for if when violent he is bound with a wild fig branch, he becomes gentle.

2.78—When they would symbolise *a man whose temperance is easily changed and inconstant*, they depict a Bull with his Right Knee Bound Round; for if you bind him by a fetter on his right knee, you will find him follow. And the bull is always assumed as a symbol of temperance, because it never approaches the cow after conception.

2.79—When they would symbolise *a slayer of sheep and goats*, they portray these Animals Eating Fleabane; for if they eat fleabane they die, being cut off by thirst.

2.80—When they would symbolise *a man eating*, they depict a Crocodile with His Mouth Open; for he ...

2.81—When they would denote *a rapacious and inactive man*, they portray a Crocodile with the Wing of an Ibis on his Head; for if you touch him with the wing of an Ibis you will find him motionless.

2.82—When they would symbolise *a woman that has brought forth once*, they depict a Lioness; for she never conceives twice.

2.83—When they would symbolise *a man born deformed at first, but that has afterwards acquired his proper shape*, they delineate a Pregnant Bear, for it brings forth (a mass of) thick and condensed blood, which is afterwards endued with life by being warmed between its thighs, and perfected by being licked with its tongue.

2.84—When they would symbolise *a powerful man, and one that discerns what things are right*, they depict an Elephant with a Trunk; for with this he discerns by smelling, and overcomes all obstacles.

2.85—When they would symbolise *a king that flees from folly and intemperance*, they delineate an Elephant and a Ram; for he flees at the sight of a ram.

2.86—When they would symbolise *a king that flees from a trifler*, they depict an Elephant with a Hog; for he flees upon hearing the voice of the hog.

2.87—When they would symbolise *a man that is quick in his movements, but who moves without prudence and consideration*, they portray a Stag and a Viper; for she flees at the sight of the viper.

2.88—When they would symbolise *a man that is providing his own tomb*, they depict an Elephant burying its own Teeth; for when his teeth fall out, he takes them up and buries them.

2.89—When they would symbolise *a man that has lived to a proper age*, they depict a Dying Crow; for she lives an hundred years according to the Egyptians; and a year among the Egyptians consists of four (of our) years.

2.90—When they would denote *a man who conceals his depravity within himself*, and hides himself so as not to be known by his own friends and family, they depict a Panther; for it secretly pursues the beasts, not suffering its scent to escape, which is [a hindrance in the pursuit?] of other animals.

2.91—When they would symbolise *a man deceived by flattery*, they represent a Stag and a Man Playing on a Pipe; for she is caught while listening to the sweet breathings of the singers as she stands entranced in pleasure.

2.92—When they would symbolise *the presage of a plentiful vintage*, they depict the Hou-Poo; for if this bird sings [moans?] before the season of the vines, it is a sign of a good vintage.

2.93—When they would symbolise *a man that is injured by the grape and cures himself*, they depict a Hou-Poo and the herb Adiantum (maidenhair); for when injured by the grape, if he places a piece of Adiantum in his mouth he is healed.

2.94—When they would symbolise *a man that guards himself from the plots of his enemies*, they depict a Crane on the Watch; for these birds guard themselves by watching in turns during the whole night.

2.95—Pædicationem designantes, geminas perdices pingunt: quæ cum viduæ sunt, se invicem abutuntur[10].

2.96—When they would symbolise *an old man dying of hunger*, they delineate an Eagle with his Beak Extremely Hooked; for as he grows old his beak becomes extremely hooked, and he dies of hunger.

2.97—When they would symbolise *a man living perpetually in motion, and agitation of mind, and not even remaining quiet during meals*, they depict the Young Ones of a Crow [a crow with its young]; for whilst she flies she feeds her young.

2.98—When they would symbolise *a man skilled in celestial matters*, they depict a Crane Flying; for she always flies very high, to inspect the clouds lest they send forth a storm, that she may remain in quiet.

2.99—When they would symbolise *a man who through want dismisses his own children*, they portray A Hawk with Egg; for though she lays three eggs, she hatches and brings up but one, and breaks the other two: and she does this on account of the loss of her claws at that season, being for that reason unable to bring up all three young ones.

2.100—When they would symbolise *a man who is tardy in moving with his feet*, they delineate a Camel; for this is the only animal which bends the thigh, whence it is called κάμηλος, a camel.

2.101—When they would symbolise *a man who is impudent and quicksighted*, they depict a Frog; for it has no blood except in the eyes alone, and they call those who have

---

[10] 'When they would symbolize pederasty they draw two partridges. For when these partners lose their mates, they make use of each other.'

blood in those parts impudent: and hence the poet sings, "Drunkard with eyes of dog and heart of stag."

2.102—When they would symbolise *a man who for a long time is unable to move himself, but who afterwards moves with his feet*, they depict a Frog having its Hind Feet; for it is born without feet, but subsequently as it grows acquires its hind feet.

2.103—When they would symbolise *a man that is hostile to, and secluded from, all men*, they depict an Eel for it is found associating with no other fishes.

2.104—When they would symbolise *a man who saves many in the sea*, they depict the Torpedo Fish; for this, when it perceives a number of fishes unable to swim, draws them to itself and preserves them.

2.105—When they would symbolise *a man that wastefully consumes both things that are requisite and useless*, they delineate a Polypus; for after eating much and extravagantly, it lays by food in its holes, and when it has consumed that which is useful, it then throws away that which is useless.

2.106—When they would symbolise *a man the ruler of his tribe*, they depict a Crayfish and a Polypus; for he rules over the polypi, and holds the chief place among them.

2.107—When they would symbolise *a man who is married to a woman from their very infancy wherein they were born*, they depict Pregnant Pinnae; for these when produced within the shell, after a short time are joined with one another, even within the shell.

2.108—When they would symbolise *a father, or a man who does not provide for himself, but is provided for by his domestics*, they depict a Pinna and a Crayfish; for this crayfish remains adhering to the flesh of the pinna, and is called pinnophylax (protector of the pinna), and acts agreeably with its name. For the pinna when hungry always opens her shell, and when, whilst she lies gaping, any little fish comes within it, the pinnophylax pinches the pinna with its claw, which when the pinna perceives, she closes her shell, and thus catches the little fish.

2.109—When they would symbolise *a man addicted to gluttony*, they delineate a Charfish; for this is the only fish which ruminates, and eats all the little fishes which fall in its way.

2.110—When they would symbolise *a man that vomits up his food, and again eats insatiably*, they depict a Seaweasel; for it brings forth through its mouth, and drinks in the seed whilst swimming.

2.111—When they would symbolise *a man that has commerce with persons of another tribe*, they depict the Lamprey; because it ascends out of the sea, and has commerce with the vipers, and straightway returns to the sea.

2.112—When they would symbolise *a man punished for murder and repenting*, they depict a Partinaca (a fish with a sting in its tail,) caught on a Hook; for when caught it casts away the sting in its tail.

2.113—When they would symbolise *a man that eats unsparingly of another's substance, and afterwards consumes his own*, they depict a Polypus; for, if he be in want of food from other things, he eats his own feelers.

2.114—When they would symbolise *a man that is eager for good, and who instead of it falls into evil*, they portray a Cuttlefish; for this fish if it see any other longing to catch it, ejects a black liquid from its belly into the water, so that by these means it is no longer visible, and thus escapes.

2.115—When they would symbolise *a prolific man*, they depict the House-Sparrow; hic enim immodicâ irâ et copiâ seminis ductus septies in horâ fœminam init copiosum semen effutiens.[11]

2.116—When they would symbolise *a man that is constant, and uniformly tempered*, they depict a Lyre; for it preserves the continuity of its notes.

2.117—When they would symbolise *a man previously deranged in his intellects, but afterwards becoming sane, and bringing a degree of regularity into his life*, they depict a Syrinx; for it is soothing, and calls to remembrance things that have been pleasurably done; and it produces a very regulated sound.

2.118—When they would symbolise *a man who distributes justice impartially to all*, they depict the Feather of an Ostrich; for this bird has the feathers of its wings equal on every side, beyond all other birds.

2.119—When they would symbolise *a man that is fond of building*, they delineate a Man's Hand; for it performs all works.

THE END OF THE HIEROGLYPHICS OF HORAPOLLO NILOUS

---

[11] 'For when the house-sparrow is driven to distraction by desire and an excess of seed, it mates with the female seven times in an hour, ejaculating all its seed at once.'

APPENDIX I

(Extracted from Giambattista della Porta; *Die Entwicklung der Emblematik*)

Die Hieroglyphica des Horapollo: Kryptographie in der Renaissance

Section 5. *Die Hieroglyphica des Horapollo*

Woher kommt die für die Renaissance typische Wertschätzung der (erst im 19. Jh. entzifferten) Geheimschrift aus dem alten Ägypten? Wir berühren hier einen mehr zeichentheoretischen Aspekt der Kryptogrammatik, der sich Gedanken darüber macht, ob es Sprachen gibt, die dem göttlichen Wort so ähnlich sind, das sie auch die Fähigkeit haben, auf die Dinge der Welt— gottgleich—gestaltend und verändernd einzuwirken. Für diese Bewertung der Hieroglyphen war die Auffindung und sofortige enthusiastische Rezeption eines Textes bedeutungsvoll: die sogenannte Hieroglyphica, eine spätantike Schrift die einem Horapollo (dem Ägyptischen Gott Horus) zugeschrieben wird. 1419 auf der Insel Andros vom Florentiner Cristoforo Buondelmonti aufgefunden ist die Hieroglyphica bis ins 17. Jh. weit verbreitet und in zahlreiche Nationalsprachen übersetzt.

Was macht diesen Text so aufsehenerregend? Die Hieroglyphica geben eine symbolische Interpretation von ca. 200 "Schriftzeichen" der Alten Ägypter: Sie sind als voneinander abgetrennte Bilder zu lesen und nicht als Elemente einer Schrift im eigentlichen Sinn. Hier ein Beispiel aus diesem eigenartigen Text: "Den Embryo bezeichnen sie mit dem Bild einer Kröte: denn seine Generation geht aus der Verfaulung der Erde hervor, d.h. aus dem Schlamm des Flusses. Und so kann man manchmal eine halb vollständigen Kröte sehen: sie ist zur einen Hälfte Lebewesen und zur anderen eine bestimmte erdhafte Sache. In der Weise, daß ohne Fluß auch keine Kröte existiert." Dieses Beispiel illustriert, was die Renaissance-Humanisten an dieser Interpretation der Hieroglyphen faszinierte: die Doktrin von der imago dissimilis, vom unähnlichen Bild scheint hier, in der Geheimsprache der ägyptischen Priester verwirklicht zu sein. In unserem Beispiel wird der Embryo wird als Kröte dargestellt, also etwas in rätselhafter (und zugleich für den Eingeweihten aufschlußreicher) Weise durch etwas anderes bezeichnet.

In diesem Zusammenhang ist es von zentraler Bedeutung, daß die Lösung des Rätsels uns wichtige Einsichten über das Werden und Vergehen organischer Lebewesen, also: in naturphilosophische Zusammenhänge vermittelt. Die Hieroglyphen sind der Idealfall einer philosophisch bedeutsamen Geheimschrift in Bildern, die — und das ist der springende Punkt—keinen direkt abbildenden Charakter haben (Embryo=Kröte). Dieser paradoxe Verweiszusammenhang setzt die Phantasie des Entschlüsselnden in Bewegung: die dabei freigesetzte psychische Energie wird zum Erlernen und Memorieren von Wissen (in unserem Beispiel über die Entstehung der Körper aus den Elementen Wasser und Erde) genutzt. Solche Einsichten in den Gang der Natur sind dann für den Adepten der ägyptischen Geheimschriftkunst in Form eines Bildes (Kröte) kurz: in Form einer ingeniösen Abbreviatur abrufbar.

Faszinierend an den Hieroglyphen ist also deren zeichentheoretisch avancierte Stellung (imago dissimilis), die den interpretierenden Betrachter miteinbezieht, sowie der pädagogische und memorative Effekt der Hieroglyphen, die als Reihen komplexer Konzepte Wissen zugänglich machen und ordnen. Gleichzeitig geht es bei den Bemühungen um die Entzifferung der Hieroglyphen um ein strategisches Wissen. Nämlich um die in der antiken Literatur (Iamblichos, Plutarch) bis hin zu Augustinus verbriefte Fähigkeit der ägyptischen Priester zur Naturbeherrschung (Athanasius Kircher). Die in der Hieroglyphica dargestellte kryptogrammatische Methode ist also in jeder Hinsicht ein für die Renaissance - Humanisten attraktives

Modell um den Inhalt ihrer religiösen, politischen, naturphilosophischen und geistigen Erfahrungen unter Eingeweihten auszutauschen.

www.ingramcontent.com/pod-product-compliance
Lightning Source LLC
Chambersburg PA
CBHW060227290526
45789CB00003B/1444